FINDING
GOD

Abiding

FINDING
GOD
Abiding

Daily Meditations

CHRISTINE MARIE EBERLE

Christine Marie Eberle

Woodhall Press | *Norwalk, CT*

*For Trish —
May
Love
Abide!*

woodhall press

Woodhall Press, 81 Old Saugatuck Road, Norwalk, CT 06855
WoodhallPress.com

"Friends Whom I Knew Not" from the volume *The Heart of God: Prayers of Rabindranath Tagore*, Selected and Edited by Herbert F. Vetter, published by Tuttle Publishing, Boston. Copyright 1997, Herbert F. Vetter. Used herewith by permission of Tuttle Publishing.

Hymn "Abide With Me" by Henry Francis Lyte, 1847. Public Domain.
Reprinted from *New Songs of Praise and Power*, Copyright 1922—Philadelphia, courtesy of www.pdinfo.com.

Cover design: Asha Hossain
Layout artist: LJ Mucci

Library of Congress Cataloging-in-Publication Data available

ISBN 978-1-954907-13-3 (paper: alk paper)
ISBN 978-1-954907-14-0 (electronic)

First Edition

Distributed by Independent Publishers Group
(800) 888-4741

Printed in the United States of America

To my grandmother, Mary Florence Reilly.

I got what I really wanted.

Contents

Part II: Becoming / 35

Part III: Embracing / 67

PART IV: RELEASING / 99

Friends Whom I Knew Not

You have made me known to friends whom I knew not. You have given me seats in homes not my own. You have brought the distant near and made a brother [or a sister] of the stranger.

I am uneasy at heart when I have to leave my accustomed shelter; I forget that there abides the old in the new and that there also You abide.

Through birth and death, in this world or in others, wherever You lead me, it is You, the same, the one Companion of my endless life, who links my heart with bonds of joy to the unfamiliar.

When one knows You, then alien there is none, then no door is shut. O grant me my prayer that I may never lose the bliss of the touch of the one in the play of the many.

—Rabindranath Tagore (1861–1941)

A God Who Abides

O f all the names for God in the religions of the world, my favorite is from the Hindu poet Rabindranath Tagore: *the one Companion of my endless life.* This captures the essence of my spirituality—the conviction that God abides with each of us as the one constant in a life marked by ceaseless change.

What does it mean to abide? Surveying dictionaries online, I found:

- to continue without fading or being lost
- to dwell
- to bear patiently
- to endure without yielding

Together, these meanings convey a sense of God's profound engagement. God chooses to dwell with each of us, a steadfast presence through life's endlessly varied ups and downs, ebbs and flows, joys and sorrows, triumphs and catastrophes.

This sense of the word appears in the poignant hymn "Abide with Me," penned by Anglican minister Henry Lyte in the nineteenth century. During his final illness, conscious of the swiftly passing days, Lyte begged the God who had been with him always to stay close by his side. The hymn begins:

> Abide with me! Fast falls the eventide,
>
> The darkness deepens—Lord, with me abide!
>
> When other helpers fail, and comforts flee,
>
> Help of the helpless, O abide with me!

Lyte's opening line alludes to the story of the road to Emmaus in Luke's Gospel. Two dejected disciples, trying to make sense of the crucifixion that seemed to have dashed all their hopes, found themselves walking and talking with the risen Jesus, with their eyes "prevented from recognizing him." Reaching their destination, but not wanting to part from this intriguing new companion, they urged him to stay. "Abide with us," they said, "for it is toward evening, and the day is far spent." Though we do not know how far spent our own days may be, like those heartbroken disciples, we often need God to help us make sense of it all.

"Abide in me as I abide in you," says Jesus in John's Gospel. The work of abiding is ours as well. Like branches on a vine, we need a mindful connection to the source of life to nourish and sustain us, helping us to grow in faith and bear good fruit.

The stories in this book are organized around four actions that run like threads through the tapestry of our lives: perceiving, becoming, embracing, and releasing. We awaken to the world around us, discover and rediscover our path, practice love in its many forms, and grieve the loss of much that we hold dear. These movements are neither sequential nor singular; we go back and forth like a weaver, creating a unique tapestry on the loom that is our life. The various givens of our arrival in this world—the accidents of genetics and geography—comprise the vertical warp strings, already in place. Between and around them, our choices and circum- stances thread the horizontal weft strings, adding pastel shades of awareness, contrasting hues of discernment, vivid colors of passion, and muted tones of grief.

Gazing too closely at the tangled threads and frayed knots of our false starts and failures, in this world we may see only the back of the tapestry. Yet God abides like a skilled weaver: moving with us, co-creating beauty, evoking meaning, and seeing the whole—of which we get mere glimpses. As Saint Paul told the Corinthians: "Now I know only in part; then I will know fully, even as I have been fully known."

You may know yourself known by this God already, in which case I hope that my musings will spark an "aha" of recognition and provoke ever-deepening insight. But if this companioning God feels to you like wishful thinking or a pleasant projection at best, I hope that you will peruse these pages with an open mind. Perhaps something you read here will tighten the warp strings for you, bringing the one Companion of *your* endless life more clearly into view.

Saint Ignatius Loyola, founder of the Jesuit order of priests and brothers, urged his followers to "find God in all things." As you ponder your own magnificent tapestry-in-progress, I pray that your ordinary days will be extraordinarily blessed by the God who abides.

PART I

PERCEIVING

You have made me known to friends whom I knew not.
You have given me seats in homes not my own.
You have brought the distant near and made a brother [or a sister] of the stranger.

—Rabindranath Tagore

H ave your eyes ever played tricks on you?

I remember opening the door to my mother one day, when I'd been expecting my aunt. Although I'd never thought they resembled each other, for one long, disorienting moment I struggled to figure out who I was looking at—my very own mother, or her sister. It was surreal.

Perceiving is a process. Even if we have perfect eyesight (or excellent corrective lenses), what we absorb still requires interpretation. If you've ever been stunned at Thanksgiving by the contrary convictions of a beloved relative, you know that two people can look at the same thing and see it very differently.

Nowhere is this more clear today than in our many fraught conversations about racism and white privilege. That thing I don't get about a Black friend's life: When does my inability to relate to her experience become a culpable unwillingness to see her reality?

Sight requires proximity, but proximity is not enough. We need insight, and insight requires vulnerability. *You have brought the distant near*, Tagore wrote, *and made a brother [or a sister] of the stranger.* God does indeed bring the distant near, opening our hearts to unfamiliar people and places, unimagined ideas, and even unexplored parts of our selves. Awareness often grows gradually, brightening as imperceptibly as dawn on an overcast day. At other times, the fog simply lifts, and we know that we will never see something the same way again.

The stories in this section explore various experiences of coming to clarity, such as practicing reflection, noticing invitations, and tolerating uncertainty. We may never be able to read the bottom line of the spiritual eye chart in this life, but one thing is certain: If we open the eyes of our heart, God will bring into our line of vision whatever we most need to see.

CHAPTER 1

Finding God without Glasses

For now we see in a mirror, dimly, but then we will see face to face.

—1 Corinthians 13:12

Reading was not Christopher's thing. When he opened a book, he didn't behold a captivating tale or a thrilling adventure; all he saw was the march of letters and the drudgery of sounding them out. Nevertheless, the summer before Christopher started kindergarten, his grandmother made it her mission to teach him to read. She tried everything, from phonics flash cards to creative word games. One afternoon, totally frustrated, young Christopher threw down his book and cried, "Why don't you just give me your *glasses?* Then I'll be able to read!"

Did the boy think his grandmother had magic glasses? Well, yes—and for good reason. Like many people of a certain age, she routinely announced, "I can't read a thing without my glasses!" Countless pairs of drugstore spectacles were stashed around the house so that she could grab them whenever she wanted to ponder a nutrition label, takeout menu, or TV listing.

No wonder Christopher was frustrated by his grandmother's insistence on teaching him to read "the hard way." All *she* had to do was put on her glasses!

Learning to read doesn't stop with the printed page. Think of all the things we have to "read" on a regular basis: tones of voice, facial expressions, body language. Employees read their bosses' mood before asking for a raise; preachers "read the room" to know when to wrap it up (or at least should).

One incident that stays with me happened at a rehearsal when two choirs came together to learn Handel's "Hallelujah Chorus." A fellow soprano whom I didn't know very well appeared to be looking daggers at me all night, sending me home awash in self-consciousness. Was I off-key? Was I too loud? Did she think I was a total diva? Later, I discovered that she was working hard to master the piece (hence, the frown) and found it helpful to watch me (hence, the staring). Gloria is a delightful woman, and I had completely misread the situation. Where are a grandmother's glasses when you need them?

Perhaps the biggest challenge to our "reading" comprehension is the story of our own life. When we look at the events of our days, from the obviously significant to the seemingly random, at first they are like a stack of notecards dropped and hastily regathered. Even when we do begin to piece our narrative together, we can still get it wrong—imagining ourselves as the main character in someone else's drama, or inaccurately casting ourselves as the hero / victim / martyr of our own.

The "glasses" we need are the ones that allow us to understand our life, not as a collection of short stories, but as part of one great mystery novel. For Christians, it's the paschal mystery: the life, death, and resurrection of Jesus, visible in our own daily dyings and risings. For everyone, it's the story of God at work—in us, and in all creation, through all time.

There are no magic glasses; we have to craft our own lenses. We do this by bringing our experiences to prayer, reflection, and conversation, by absorbing the wisdom of Scripture and tradition, and by charting the faltering steps and surprising leaps of our own spiritual growth, until we can see that the story of our life is really a story of God's grace.

If you possessed spiritual "magic glasses," what memory or current dilemma would you most want to look at? What question(s) would you ask God about the story of your life?

CHAPTER 2

Finding God in a Spiral-Bound Notebook

Regard the patience of our Lord as salvation.

—2 Peter 3:15

I've been a dogged journal-keeper for most of my adult life. It's not a daily ritual; sometimes weeks or occasionally months elapse, but I always return to the practice. When I reach the end of one book, I usually keep it nearby so I can reread it as a New Year's or birthday activity, after which my collected musings join their predecessors in a big box under my bed. Occasionally, though, something will send me rummaging through those old spiral-bound volumes, and I wind up drawn into a lengthy reading session right there on the bedroom floor. Inevitably, what I find falls into one of three categories.

Most unnerving are the "black hole" items. In my first semester of college, for example, it seems I went to the gym a few times with someone from my poetry class. I remember the class, can't quite picture the girl, and have no recollection of ever setting sneaker in that gym. Things that must have been significant are simply lost in space—such as vigorous debates with people whose last names I did not record because they were so evident at the time. Ironically, there may be good news buried here as well: perhaps today's all-consuming crisis will not leave so much as a footprint in my memory.

Next are the stories that make me breathe a sigh of relief, realizing how far I've come: florid accounts of romances pursued or thwarted, dramatic retellings of interpersonal conflicts, and confessional narratives of demons long since wrestled to the ground. Rereading these, I am awash in gratitude for the relative peace within and around me now. It is helpful to remember that things really can change . . . that *I* really can change. There's nothing like a good dose of perspective to give us confidence for the road ahead.

And yet, there are also entries that make me wonder if that road is just one long loop. In them, I berate myself for my critical spirit and sharp tongue. I marvel at the restorative power of a day alone and wonder why I don't give my soul the rest it needs more often. I reach the startling conclusion that the only person setting the bar so high I can't reach it is *me*. If it didn't have a date at the top, I would have no clue that I was reading something from decades ago.

It is tempting to be discouraged by that third category. How can a person so committed to spiritual growth keep getting an "improvement needed" mark on her divine report card? The answer, of course, is that "God-as-disappointed-schoolmarm" lives only in my imagination: the childish caricature of a stern deity.

Rereading the journal I kept when I made the *Spiritual Exercises* of Saint Ignatius Loyola in my mid-thirties, I see once again how I came to understand myself as a loved sinner whose imperfections were the countless cracks through which the light of God could shine. The persistence of some of those imperfections does not have to be a source of shame, even now.

I am a slow learner, loved by a patient teacher. God's compassionate abiding enriches my life far more than any elusive perfect score.

Find some record of your earlier self. It could be a journal entry, a letter that has come back into your keeping, or even a childhood photo. Pray with it, noticing both surprising growth and stubborn flaws. What does your loving, patient Teacher want you to see?

CHAPTER 3

Finding God in the Middle

Give me neither poverty nor riches; feed me with the food that I need,
or I shall be full, and deny you, and say, "Who is the Lord?"
or I shall be poor, and steal, and profane the name of my God.

—Proverbs 30:8–9

"How can I feel so miserably poor and embarrassingly rich at the same time?" my cousin Susan lamented. She and her young daughters had just finished a play date at a friend's suburban mansion, and she was awash in envy. Oh, to have a whole finished basement for toys and art supplies, instead of tripping over dollhouse furniture in the living room and shifting still-wet masterpieces from the dinner table! How luxurious to be able to send children out to play in a fenced-in half-acre! Susan's row home had only a scrap of back yard on the far side of a common driveway; she couldn't leave her kids unattended for a minute.

Feeling dispirited about her little house and wishing she could give her girls more, Susan ran into a neighbor—a young mother who lived in the apartment building next door. A recent Ukrainian immigrant, this neighbor shared her small basement apartment with a large extended family, and she had a favor to ask. "Could I bring my daughter over to play in your yard sometimes? She is just learning to walk, and it is so nice to have a bit of grass!"

Was Susan poor or was she rich? The truth is, she was neither—simply better off than some, worse off than others in our mixed-income borough. That's why she simultaneously could be envious of the friend who'd never had to watch every penny, and grateful to have so many pennies to watch.

Susan's pithy summary of her dilemma perfectly captures my own conflicted thoughts about money over the years. I remember, especially in my "salad days" (peanut butter and ramen days, more precisely), gazing at people with luxurious possessions and imagining that their wealth insulated them from unhappiness. Someone once described that train of thought as "comparing your insides to other people's outsides," a phenomenon only intensified these days by all those carefully crafted Instagram posts.

Most of us are rich in something: if not money, then friends, time, talent, creativity, love, etc. Figuring out what we have to share—as Susan shared her tiny back yard with her immigrant neighbor—connects us to the source of our abundance. No matter where I have been on the financial spectrum, identifying my own *plenty* has grounded me in gratitude and freed me to be generous—even on the days when I couldn't afford to replace two tissue boxes at once.

Similarly, most of us experience some form of poverty unrelated to our bank balance. I sing for my church, for example, but I can't read music; I'm a mother figure to many, but I've never borne a child. Nonmaterial poverty could include an insufficiency of contentment, an absence of charity, or a tendency to choose self-protection over self-sacrifice. Perhaps we are financially comfortable, but emotionally guarded; that too is a poverty. Recognizing this keeps us humble, conscious of our interdependence.

In the end, rich or poor, it's not about what we have or what we lack. It's about how we harden or soften our hearts toward those with less—or more.

In a spirit of prayer, try making two lists. How are you rich? Where are you poor? Ask God to show you what you are called to give—and receive.

CHAPTER 4

Finding God in a Fire Siren

Lord, teach us to pray.

—Luke 11:1

"There's no reason for them to blow that siren anymore," my neighbor insisted. "Everyone has pagers now."

The volunteer fire station is less than a hundred yards from our bedroom windows. At all times of the day and night, its powerful siren cranks up to a sustained, nerve-jangling pitch, wakening babies and generally shattering the peace. Why should we put up with this blasted racket, he went on, when there was a nondisruptive alternative? Would I join him at the upcoming town meeting to help make his case?

This was not just any neighbor, but the one we called "the mayor of the block." Retired yet busy, Albert kept tabs on everyone. He was incredibly helpful, full of generous energy. The morning after any winter storm, there he would be, using his snowblower to clear the sidewalk on both sides of the block. Once—in the cold, without gloves—he took a saw to a tree that had fallen across our driveway, just so I could get to work. He was a person on whom I had come to rely. Now, he was asking me for something. And I was going to have to refuse.

It's funny, the things that push us to take a stand. Despite being in my neighbor's debt—despite Albert's genuine concern for the jangled nerves and wakened babies of our block—there was no way I could oppose the fire siren. I couldn't even give the sort of noncommittal response that would allow him to *think* that I agreed, but (alas) just couldn't make the meeting.

"I'm sorry," I said. "I can't. My mother always told me that when I hear a siren, it means someone is in trouble, and someone is going to help, and since neither of those people is *me*, the least I can do is stop and pray for them." To this, the mayor of the block had no response (though he may have added "religious nut" to his mental file on me).

For decades now, the sound of a siren has prompted me to say a Hail Mary, but I can dash off a rote prayer without breaking my stride. While dog-sitting recently, however, I was humbled in this regard by a springer spaniel named Duncan. Upon hearing the siren while trotting happily along on a walk, Duncan froze, shot me a perplexed look, then threw back his head and howled. Pure instinct, no doubt, but to me it looked like the sort of full-throated prayer the situation actually deserved.

Each day contains countless opportunities to raise our minds and hearts to God, especially once we decide to notice a thing: the coo of a mourning dove or the whistle of a train; a glimpse of a bright red poppy or a postal worker on her appointed rounds; a rainbow in the sky or one at our feet in sidewalk chalk. Prayer turns us toward God, like sunflowers to the light. Anything that invites us to *pause* can be as sacred as a cathedral door.

"Pray for me!" we often say in times of trouble. I like to think of the fire siren as just that: our first responders' dashed-off plea as they race to someone's assistance. I'm glad the siren continues to disrupt my peace, so I can pray for theirs. Perhaps my neighbors are doing that as well: encircling them in prayers for protection, despite occasional grumbles about the noise.

What prompts you to prayer now? Would you consider adding something else? It could be as ordinary as the dryer buzzer. Anything you choose can become your personal call to prayer, summoning you to mindfulness.

CHAPTER 5

Finding God without a Place to Sleep

You shall not wrong or oppress a resident alien, for you were aliens in the land of Egypt.

—Exodus 22:21

I recall almost nothing about the conference. I couldn't tell you the year, location, or topic; I can only narrow it down to "more than thirty years ago, on a college campus—something to do with homelessness." The one thing I do remember is this: When I arrived at the registration table, they were not yet clear about my housing. Nonchalantly, they suggested I go enjoy the keynote address and check back later.

Everything else from that weekend has evaporated from my mind like rain on a hot pavement, but the memory of not knowing where I was going to sleep that night is lodged in my gut. Though not a particularly anxious person, I was consumed by the uncertainty; I couldn't focus on the opening speaker or make even casual conversation with the people at my table.

In retrospect, I realize this was probably the first time I'd experienced any threat to my basic needs. And let's be clear—it wasn't that big a threat. They hadn't said they didn't know *if* I'd have a bed for the night, only *where*. Nevertheless, until the question was resolved, I was incapable of going beyond myself. I was a mess.

If something like that happened today, I'm sure I'd roll with it better, starting by appreciating the irony of being without a bed at a conference on homelessness, then holding the unknowns of the night more loosely. Of course, I'd also be holding a credit card, a thing I did not have back then. (Several years later, in fact, a girlfriend and I were briefly unsheltered when we arrived at Boston's Logan Airport to find all flights home canceled until morning. We wound up tracking down a friend with an extra bedroom, but having a credit card made the whole thing a lark rather than a crisis.)

The lesson I draw from these memories is not about managing uncertainty, however, but about experiencing empathy. Although I have learned many things over the years about the psychology of people in need, what remains most instructive is the recollection of my obliterating anxiety in the opening hours of that conference. When it is tempting to gaze with middle-class condescension at the poor decisions of a person whose basic needs are forever in jeopardy, remembering how undone I was that night curbs my rush to judgment.

I find it intriguing that God's initial ethical instruction about how to treat strangers was grounded in exactly this kind of recollection: Do not oppress an alien, for you were aliens once yourselves. In other words, do unto others as you wish they had done unto you. This golden rule variation would be good to remember when the descendants of people thwarted by "Irish need not apply" signs are making hiring decisions about applicants with darker skin, distracting tattoos, or distinctive religious attire.

It is essential that those of us who are generally comfortable go out of our way to be in uncomfortable situations and then reflect on the experience. Feeling what it's like to be the outsider—the one lacking the knowledge, skills, language, ingenuity, connections, or other resources to glide effortlessly through a situation—can give us a more lasting dose of compassion than a dozen articles we might read on the topic.

Sometimes, before we can train our vision, we need to retrain our hearts.

When have you been an "alien," even temporarily? How can you use that experience to summon empathy for people who are outsiders in some significant way?

CHAPTER 6

Finding God without Comparing

God saw everything that he had made, and indeed, it was very good.

—Genesis 1:31

"I t's Teeny-Weeny String Beanie!" When I was a child, that's what my Uncle Bob would exclaim whenever I arrived at his house. ("Teen" was my family nickname; the embellishment was all Uncle Bob.) It's not that I was a particularly skinny kid; I think he just liked the rhyme. Remembering those affectionate greetings now, what really moves me—besides how much I adored my uncle, who died when I was twenty-eight—is that I experienced no separation between how I felt about myself and how I felt about my body. We were one. One teeny-weeny string beanie, source of joy.

When did that unselfconscious delight stop? At puberty, I presume; certainly by college. Ever since, it's been me vs. my body: often at war, rarely at peace, only recently in uneasy alliance. Whether the topic *du jour* is my weight (fluctuating) or my shape (pear, unfluctuating) or my height (lacking) or my thighs (don't get me started), never do I look in the mirror and think, *Yes! You look good, girl! Now go think about something else.*

The problem, I tell myself, is other people's bodies. If only I didn't have a steady supply of comparison, all around me and on every screen I see, perhaps I could forget to be self-conscious about my own flesh for half a minute.

Is it like this for all of us? Upon spotting another body similar to our own, does everyone automatically register the differences first? I imagine the criteria for judgment vary: slimmer or broader, lighter or darker, more or less toned, groomed, endowed . . . you fill in the blank. I remember talking with my cousin Susan (taller, thinner) about women who looked so put-to-gether: brows shaped, nails lacquered, hair styled, makeup applied, Spanx on, heels high. Their beauty was as baffling as it was mesmerizing. Batting around in gardening clothes and ponytails, we "crunchy granola" gals couldn't fathom how to achieve that look—and didn't actually want to—yet we couldn't look away.

A few years ago, I had an aha moment reading Rev. Kate Braestrup's memoir, *Here If You Need Me*. A chaplain to the Maine Warden Service, Reverend Braestrup explains why she chooses not to wear her department-issued Kevlar vest—potentially handy in the woods during hunting season. "People hug me," she says. "My body needs to be soft and squishy."

That is so beautifully grounded. Reverend Braestrup is neither dismissing her body nor aiming for the level of fitness her muscular colleagues display. Rather, she sees her body as useful and comforting. I find that so . . . useful and comforting. Although I try to make good choices around eating and exercise, deep down I recognize that *how I look* has never been synonymous with *who I am*. In my mid-fifties now, I want a body that works, and welcomes, and doesn't require a lot of high maintenance to stay that way.

I do not want to reach the metaphorical pearly gates and have to account for years of my life spent judging my body harshly. I'd rather hear Uncle Bob exclaim, "It's Teeny-Weeny String Beanie!" Then I want God to gather me into those divine arms and croon the words of another Reverend—Mr. Rogers: "I like you just the way you are."

If you struggle with body image, imagine God holding (or beholding) you, and saying those immortal words of Mr. Rogers. What shifts in you? Can you say them to yourself?

Chapter 7

Finding God in the Everlasting Tide

Lord, you have been our dwelling place in all generations.

—Psalm 90:1

The summer I turned five, I went on my first extended-family vacation to Wildwood, New Jersey, where we'd booked a one-bedroom motel room for four nights. While my father and uncle stayed home to work, five of us piled into my aunt Eileen's Chevy Nova: Eileen and her son, Michael, my mom and me, and our recently widowed grandmother. Mike and I played in the ocean until our lips turned blue, ate sandy peanut butter crackers with black-and-white milkshakes for lunch, and tried all the kiddie rides on the boardwalk. It was the best week of my life (to that point).

The family pilgrimage to Wildwood has continued for more than fifty summers now, although the cast of characters has shifted with every milestone event. After several years in motels, we switched to an apartment, then a condo, then several. During the expansion phase, air mattresses covered the floors; at our peak ratio of bodies to beds, under-the-dining-room-table and in-the-master-bedroom-closet were official sleep spots. My cousins' Legos and sand toys yielded to guitars and Rollerblades, replaced by fancier Legos and bigger sand toys as those cousins had kids of their own.

My brother refers to our time at the shore as the "annual family snapshot." (Not literally; we tried that once, and it was like getting feral cats to strike a pose.) Now that we are distanced by geography and commitments, the shore is the primary place we connect—going for long bike rides in the morning, sitting in a big circle on the beach in the afternoon, and enjoying boisterous card games at night. Reading about someone's children in a Christmas letter or getting a job update at a birthday party is no substitute for those precious days of shared life.

The shore has become an annual snapshot of my spirit as well. How many profound conversations have I had, walking along that surf line? How many big decisions have I prayed about, gazing out over those waves? I look around and see myself at every age: antsy child, awkward adolescent, searching young adult, grieving forty-something. The week is awash in traditions, memories, and oft-told tales, making the veil separating us from our beloved deceased feel reassuringly thin. The shore is a touchstone—a place and a time where the past is present.

In the family, different summers have been dominated by diapers, or teenagers, or Alzheimer's, but every August—no matter what is going on in our lives or in the world—most of us make our way to Wildwood. The essentials have never changed, and I take comfort in that.

On the island, though neon-lit motels and weathered beach shacks have made way for fancy townhouses and condo complexes, the sun still rises over the ocean and sets into the bay; the waves crest and crash; the seagulls laugh, and the piping plovers run. It even smells the same.

Returning to this place helps me step back from the tapestry of daily life—the place where my nose is pressed up against the present—and see the pattern that has emerged over time. In the wake of much loss, the shore is a potent reminder of God's abiding love: constant as the everlasting tide.

What connects you to earlier versions of yourself? It could be a place, an experience, a taste, a smell. In prayer, let your imagination take you back, following that thread through the seasons of your life. How has God been present, constant as the tide?

Part II

Becoming

I am uneasy at heart when I have to leave my accustomed shelter;
I forget that there abides the old in the new and that there also You abide.

—Rabindranath Tagore

What did you want to be when you grew up?

If you'd asked me that question as a child, I'd have said that I wanted to be an astronaut, a ballerina, or a writer. Enjoying *Star Trek* and a good Pilates class is as close as I got to the first two. I did become a writer, obviously—though not a novelist, as I first envisioned.

Think back to your own childhood imaginings. Were any seeds planted then that are flourishing now? How would you answer the "what do you want to be" question today?

Few people can draw a straight line from youthful fantasy to adult paycheck; most of us take a meandering path toward fulfillment. My father wanted to be a train engineer when he was little, but after high school he went to seminary, then changed his mind and became an accountant. In his early forties, a downsizing at his company inspired him to try teaching economics—a career he wound up loving for more than thirty years. I picture my young father walking dejectedly out the seminary gates for the last time, uncertain of his future; could he have imagined that his defining work was still two decades away?

My father's story illustrates how the question of vocation can add a layer of pressure to life decisions. On the one hand, there is the excitement of listening for God's voice; on the other, the fear of missing the call (so to speak). To paraphrase Tagore, *we forget that there abides the old in the new, and there also God abides.*

The stories in this section capture several pivot points in my own evolving self-understanding: my initial wonderment about a religious vocation; choosing and re-choosing a major; surviving professional detours and personal upheavals—all while trying to be attentive to God's desire for my life.

The problem with asking what we want to be when we grow up is twofold. First, the question equates *being* with *doing*, when we are so much more than what we do, especially for a living. Also, the question implies a static answer, when we are never just one thing. Our lives continue to unfold in surprising ways, right up to our last breath.

What do we want to be? Through the grace of God, we are always becoming.

CHAPTER 8

Finding God by Another Way

Then, being divinely warned in a dream that they should not return to Herod,
[the Magi] departed for their own country by another way.

—Matthew 2:12

"Oh, rats! I think I'm supposed to be a nun."

I was kneeling in the chapel balcony at the Mercy Motherhouse, where my eighth-grade teacher had brought us for retreat. Praying earnestly, I was thunderstruck by the conviction that, because God had given me many gifts, I was obliged to use them in God's service as a religious sister. I wasn't happy about it; I'd been dreaming of marriage and a family since my first crush in kindergarten. Unfortunately, I was pretty sure God's will for my life had just been revealed.

I kept those thoughts at bay through high school and well into college, but as the time approached to decide what to do after graduation, they politely raised their hand again. I wasn't a bookish eighth grader anymore; I was about to be a bona fide (young) adult with a theology degree. Maybe I really was supposed to be a nun. I wasn't any more enthusiastic; my high school boyfriend had also raised *his* hand again. Nevertheless, I started the process of inquiry.

I knew I didn't want to be a nurse or a teacher (classic nun jobs), but I'd heard that the Dominican sisters did retreat work, so I began going on "come and see" weekends and having soul-searching conversations with their vocation director. After many months of this, Sister Maria said something that shocked me. "It is very clear that you are called to this work," she mused, "but it is much less clear that you are called to this *life*. You might have to find another way to do the work."

Wait. There was another way to do the work?

My imagination had been limited by my experience. This was Philadelphia in the '80s; compared to other parts of the country, we still had an abundance of sisters and priests. "Lay ministry" would have sounded like an oxymoron, if I'd even heard the term. But Sister Maria was clear, and she was prophetic. I did, in fact, find another way to do the work—many ways, in fact.

Later, I learned the *Suscipe*—the prayer of surrender—of Saint Ignatius Loyola: "Take, Lord, and receive all my liberty, my memory, my understanding, and my entire will, all that I have and call my own. You have given all to me. To you, Lord, I return it."

To you, Lord, I return it. That is exactly what eighth-grade me was trying to express, though I didn't have the words yet. I knew that everything I had was from God. I did not yet know that everything I *was* could be entrusted to God, who would not call me to anything for which I was unsuited.

The specificity of my response wasn't nearly as important as the orientation of my heart, because what I experienced in that chapel balcony was not a marching order, but the beginning of a conversation. I had no idea how the desire sparked there—to serve God in gratitude—would work itself out over the course of subsequent decades. And I still don't know, fully, because a surprising life turn could be as close as the next phone call.

Take, Lord, receive.

Whenever I read the Scripture passage that opens this chapter, I love that the Magi headed home "by another way." Faced with an unnerving obstacle, they weren't thwarted; they just pivoted. As you consider the uncertainties of your own future, how would a wholehearted prayer of surrender affect your feelings about the path ahead?

CHAPTER 9

Finding God for All the Wrong Reasons

For surely I know the plans I have for you, says the Lord,
plans for your welfare and not for harm, to give you a future with hope.

—Jeremiah 29:11

Despite wondering about a religious vocation at the end of eighth grade, nothing about my teenage years suggested a career in ministry. In high school, I didn't join the community service corps, sing in the choir, or serve as a chapel aide like some of my friends. All I ever wanted to do was read and write. I chose English as my college major, hoping that editing books by day and crafting them by night could leverage my two loves into one modest income—at least until I published my first bestselling novel.

Unfortunately, my freshman year was fairly miserable. I was an introverted commuter, working part-time at a bakery and driving my little brother to nursery school each day so I could have the car. I didn't join any activities or make a single friend.

At the beginning of sophomore year, however, I was chatting with my advisor outside his office when the editor of the campus literary magazine walked by. "You two should know each other," Dr. Gilman said, so I exchanged pleasantries with a dreamy-looking senior named Jim. A few days later, I spotted Jim outside the cafeteria, working the sign-up table for a weekend getaway in beautiful Cape May, New Jersey. He was dashing. I loved the shore. And oh, by the way, it was a religious retreat. Motivated by those three things—in that order—I registered on the spot.

No, in case you're wondering: Girl met boy, but girl didn't even come close to getting boy. Jim was already dating the love of his life and is married to her still. Cheesy as it sounds, however, that retreat did change my life. It introduced me to campus ministry, plunged me into a community of like-minded friends, and began to transform my understanding of faith. As a junior, I began double-majoring in theology. By senior year, I was researching graduate schools and reimagining my career trajectory, eventually spending twenty-six years as a campus minister. Writing continued to be an essential component of my work, but in a context more satisfying than I'd ever envisioned.

In the movie *Sliding Doors*, Gwyneth Paltrow's character experiences two dramatically different futures based on the simple happenstance of catching or missing one train. What would my future have held, had a random hallway encounter not drawn me through the doorway to ministry? When I think of that passing crush now, I picture God delightedly plotting how to capture my attention. I'm not suggesting that I was duped into pursuing a path I never would have chosen, like a striped bass chasing a nice minnow and winding up in a nice lemon garlic sauce instead. It's just that I'd been following the only road I knew until an attractive stranger (sent by God, I trust) turned my head and set me off in a new direction.

If we believe that God created us, it makes sense that God would know how best to lead us toward our true vocation—a full and fulfilling life. In order to get us to bite, however, God may have to lure us with a tasty morsel or two. This is not trickery and deceit, but simply a manifestation of love from the One who knows us far better than we know ourselves.

Did you get where you are today by any curious twists or turns? What first lured you in that direction? Smile at the loving cleverness of our God, whose handiwork is most often visible in retrospect.

CHAPTER 10

Finding God in Small Things

It is the smallest of all the seeds, but when it has grown it is the greatest of shrubs.

—Matthew 13:32

A graduate student with a wedding ring was hit by a car on the sidewalk, rushed to the emergency room, and whisked into surgery. As the chaplain on call, I had the heartbreaking task of helping an ER nurse locate Simon's next of kin—before cell phones, without the internet. Inside his backpack was an address book with neatly penciled contacts. The nurse began calling people with Simon's last name, frightening his grandmother in Wisconsin before reaching his wife, Maggie, at work.

This trauma hit me hard, no doubt because I could relate to the victim. Simon was a young married person (as I was) walking down a University City street (as I often did). Even though the ICU where they brought him after surgery was not on one of my floors, I couldn't stay away. Unable to help Simon, I desperately wanted to comfort his wife. In a brief bedside visit the next morning, I told her about going through the backpack, and how its contents revealed some lovely, quirky things about her husband's personality.

When I slipped into the family waiting room to say good-bye at the end of the day, Maggie asked if I could do her a favor.

My heart leaped; yes, anything!

"Can you find Simon's cross for me?"

That wasn't how I'd been hoping to minister to Maggie when I first walked into the ICU. As a chaplain in training, I imagined having a heartfelt talk, holding her while she sobbed, or praying together for Simon's healing. Yet that's not what Maggie needed. What she needed was a small thing—a beloved object she feared was gone for good.

I went to the storage closet, rummaged through Simon's belongings, and found the reddish cross the nurse had been clutching as she'd made those phone calls.

I was almost back to the room when the color registered. I bit my lip, found a sink, and washed Simon's blood from the gleaming gold, drying it carefully so Maggie wouldn't suspect the trick.

"Thank you," she said. "You've been super."

The next morning, I learned that Simon had passed overnight.

In her memoir, *This Flowing Toward Me: A Story of God Arriving in Strangers*, Sister of Mercy Marilyn Lacey defines mercy as "responding in practical ways to needs that are known." Knowing requires noticing, and I believe that's the small gift I was able to give Maggie that day.

I had paid attention to the details of Simon's book bag. I knew where his cross was. I knew (just in time) why it was red. I knew Maggie didn't need that visceral reminder of her husband's trauma. And I responded, simply and mercifully.

My moments with Maggie helped me to learn something about myself as a chaplain—and as a person. When someone is grieving, the simplest deeds have the power to move and comfort. Those who would offer consolation don't have to chew up the scenery with an exaggerated show of support. If we draw close, keep quiet, pay attention, then do whatever loving task presents itself, we can trust that God will use us for good.

Can you think of a small kindness that consoled you during a painful time? Who do you know who is suffering now? In prayer, allow the particulars of their need to surface. What do you notice? How might you respond, simply and quietly?

CHAPTER 11

Finding God in a Warm Gyro

For the gifts and the calling of God are irrevocable.

—Romans 11:29

The tantalizing aroma arrested our steps in front of a Greek restaurant on South Street, where we were searching for dinner one summer evening. Just inside the open front window, cooks were shaving slices of meat from a glowing rotisserie of lamb, preparing mouthwatering gyros.

After we placed our order, my mood plummeted. I couldn't stop staring at that spool of meat. It felt like an apt—though unfortunate—metaphor for my life.

After college, I had spent a year working in a house of hospitality for people experiencing homelessness, then I'd gotten married, gone to grad school, and completed a year of clinical training as a hospital chaplain. With my husband in law school, it was my turn to take the financial reins. I needed employment, *pronto*, but couldn't find anything in ministry. A friend had a serendipitous job opening, which is how I found myself—an aspiring campus minister in my mid-twenties—working as an executive secretary at a health insurance company.

It wasn't a bad job. My boss and I had a fantastic working relationship. The hours, salary, and benefits were generous. My coworkers were friendly, and I didn't take my work home with me. Nevertheless, the distance between where I was and where I'd hoped to be was devastating. I was sliding into a depression that seemed to intensify every time someone asked me what I *did*. I felt like that rotisserie lamb—more and more of the real "me" getting shaved away until my old self was unrecognizable.

To this day, I have such mixed feelings about that chapter in my life. I have tremendous respect for administrative assistants—still the unsung heroes of so many workplaces. The fact that I was embarrassed to be among their number is, itself, embarrassing. I believe that a job done kindly and well is a thing to be proud of, as each of us does our bit for the reign of God. Perhaps that was the trouble, though—it didn't feel like *my* bit.

Once I was a campus minister, I always encouraged students to listen for God's call, to choose something meaningful that fit their talents and aspirations, and not to trade self-discovery for the promise of financial security. *Follow your dreams*, I urged them. And yet, so many essential jobs—including the ones that put food on families' tables—are not anyone's dream. Where would we be if no one did them?

The truth is, tremendous good came from my time as an executive secretary. I made lasting friendships, gained valuable work skills, wrote my master's thesis, and even had time for weekly volunteer work. God wastes nothing. Purpose comes in countless forms.

Perhaps folk singer Charlie King said it best: *Our life is more than our work, and our work is more than our job.* During the secretarial years, any fidelity I showed to the life and the work right in front of me was, in fact, a response to God's call. More importantly, my value as a child of God—not to mention as a wife, daughter, sister, and friend—was never diminished like that rotisserie lamb. I only thought it was.

God doesn't call us just once, or in just one way. The invitations pour into our spiritual mailbox, awaiting our wholehearted response each day.

Ponder the lyric, "Our life is more than our work, and our work is more than our job," and imagine the concentric circles of your job, your work, and your life. How do you respond to God's call within each of those circles?

CHAPTER 12

Finding God from the Boiler Room

O LORD, how long shall I cry for help, and you will not listen?

—Habakkuk 1:2

When I finally landed the job of my dreams in campus ministry, my joy was quickly tempered. I worked for a priest who eventually was subject to a grand jury investigation. Though not guilty of the appalling offenses revealed by the clergy scandal, he nevertheless was found "unsuitable for ministry."

Red flags were apparent almost at once. I knew I had to do something, but I was conscious of how little credibility I had as a twenty-something woman in her first church job. Summoning my courage, I wrote a strongly worded appeal to the diocese. I read my letter to a friend, who said, "You know this may get *you* fired, right?"

Into the mailbox it went.

It took ten months and many tense phone calls, but finally there came a Friday when—my colleague out of the country on vacation—two priests from the clergy office arrived to interview me and gather evidence. I spent the weekend pacing, soaked in dread, pondering my fate. A quite uncharacteristic thought jogged through my prayer: *God, maybe you really are male, and on their side, and I'm about to lose the job I worked so hard to get.*

When the call finally came, it was not to announce my dismissal, but to appoint me acting director. My boss was removed from his position, effective immediately. Two months later, the Archdiocese assigned a genuine, faith-filled priest to the position, and we had a wonderful collaboration for the next ten years.

Later, when one of our graduates was about to accept her first job in ministry, our handyman (a former navy man) half-jokingly told her, "Watch out! The view from the boiler room isn't nearly as pretty as the one from the deck."

Pleading for justice with diocesan officials had been a real "boiler room" experience—a dark and distressing year that often left me drenched in sweat. Like a ship's boiler room, however, the ordeal had fueled my forward momentum. Heading into the next academic year, I wasn't just a "twenty-something woman in her first church job." My pastoral identity was clear: I knew beyond a doubt that I was entrusted with the care of souls and the cultivation of a faith community on that campus.

Still, my quiver of doubt during that long-ago weekend showed me how easily someone's faith can unravel. What if the clergy office had *not* done right by me? Would that have meant that God was male, and on their side? A quarter of a century later, it is easy for me to say no, of course not. But it would not have felt that way at the time. My heart aches for those who seek, knock, ask, yet hear nothing, or who bear the weight of indignities made heavier by the actions—and inaction—of people in power, straining belief in a just God.

It strikes me that the only way to assure someone of God's abiding care is to model it. In this, I'm sure I fail repeatedly. How could I not? So I take to heart these words from the Jewish Mishnah: "You are not obligated to complete the work, but neither are you free to abandon it."

What strains your belief in a just God? Is there an unanswered prayer or persistent injustice—personal, societal, or global—that weighs on you? Can you talk to God about this? (Is there someone else you feel drawn to talk with?) Try imagining God standing by your side, seeing what you see. What might God want you to know, or to do?

CHAPTER 13

Finding God Alone

Search me, O God, and know my heart; test me and know my thoughts.

—Psalm 139:23

When I was thirty, after several years of increasing strife between us, my husband took a job on the other side of the globe, and I found myself living alone for the first time. Closing the door to an apartment that was only mine, I breathed a sigh of relief. I'd heard the expression, "Peace is more than just the absence of conflict," but, for the moment, the absence of conflict was enough.

Immediately, I became very focused on living alone *well*. I wasn't going to be one of those single ladies with nothing in her shopping cart but seven Lean Cuisines, a gallon of ice cream, and a case of cat food. I was going to cook healthy meals, read good literature, and keep my home clean and serene. I was going to have quality prayer time Every Single Day.

I spent the first few months with an imaginary camera trained on myself, monitoring my every move. In the words of C. S. Lewis in *Surprised by Joy*, "I stood anxious sentinel at my own mind." Was I spending my mornings prayerfully enough? Was I passing my evenings meaningfully enough? Was I using this gift of time and space productively enough, or just frittering it away?

Though I believe in the value of personal reflection, there is a big difference between regularly taking an honest look at myself before God and what I was doing in that first year alone: ceaselessly self-monitoring according to my own unrealistic standards.

Even after the initial angst died down—after I was divorced, and my marriage annulled—I continued to second-guess myself. I remember feeling a wave of contentment one Sunday evening as I curled up with a cup of tea to watch a taped episode of *The West Wing*, my cats draped on the futon behind me. Immediately, a doubting thought crashed the party. *Sure, this is nice tonight. But if this is how you're spending your Sunday evenings a decade from now, how will you feel then?* (In retrospect, "delighted that *The West Wing* is in season ten" would have been the right answer.)

It has come to my attention that not everyone experiences this relentless internal critic. Nevertheless, I think the inability to feel "good enough" afflicts many people—including creative types, helping professionals, and most parents. Even Jan Richardson, one of my favorite contemporary spiritual writers, confesses in her beautiful grief memoir, *Sparrow*: "I look at what I've written here and worry if it's enough. And what kind of question is that? What would *enough* look like or feel like?" (Tell me if you figure it out, Jan; I'd love to know.)

What is the remedy for all this anxious striving? I believe the opposite movement is not complacency, but gratitude. When we find ourselves lacking, summoning grateful awareness of all we have and all we *are* is a keen antidote. Interestingly, in the daily Consciousness Examen (Saint Ignatius Loyola's spin on the examination of conscience), "reflective thanksgiving" is the step *before* "practical survey of actions." Starting our self-examination with gratitude stirs up love, dissipates fear, allows us to see God's hand more clearly, and enables us to face tomorrow with humble confidence.

Enough. Enough.

In what area of your life are you afflicted by worries of being "not enough"? Spend some time in prayer naming every cause for gratitude, even there. How does being steeped in gratefulness shift your thinking?

CHAPTER 14

Finding God in a Plumber's Wrench

For my thoughts are not your thoughts, nor are your ways my ways, says the Lord.

—Isaiah 55:8

T he biggest problem with having unauthorized cats is that you can't call the landlord.
My lease said "No pets," but a charming stray had selected me as her new roommate, and then she birthed kittens under my bed. Predictably, I kept the runt. While having two cats technically made me a bad tenant, it also made me an easy one: I paid the rent on time and never asked for anything. This arrangement usually worked well for all of us, but now my kitchen sink was leaking, and I was going to have to fix a broken pipe myself.

Unfortunately, this was before YouTube gave us the ability to type "How do I . . ." and watch a simple instructional video on just about any topic. Fortunately, I had something even better: an independent hardware store in walking distance, complete with helpful owner. Over the course of a long and frustrating Saturday afternoon, I visited his store at least three times for advice, replacement pipe, plumber's tape, and increasingly larger tools. He sold me a good wrench to replace my dopey little one, but the nut I was trying to turn still wouldn't budge. Maybe I needed an even bigger wrench?

I went back to the store, and he *loaned* me one. ("Seriously," he said. "Just bring it back when you're done.") Kneeling on the kitchen floor, I leaned on that thing with all my might. The nut stayed put. The tool slipped. I pitched forward, slammed my head against the cabinet, and burst out crying.

Pulling myself together, I took my borrowed wrench and sad tale back to the hardware store. The owner looked at me incredulously, like he'd loaned me a machete and I still couldn't get an envelope open with it. Suddenly, he cocked his head. "Which direction are you trying to turn the nut?"

Aha.

Sheepishly, I trudged home, removed the nut, replaced the pipe, and practically skipped back to return the wrench and pledge my undying customer loyalty.

All my life, I'd been taught that the solution to any problem was to *try harder*. With the notable exception of marriage counseling, that mind-set had served me well. It had gotten me through AP Bio in high school, probability and statistics in college, and database management in campus ministry. Just try harder; it was practically my motto. And, in this case, it was literally counterproductive: Turning that nut in the wrong direction—no matter how hard I tried—was never going to work.

How do we know when it's time to try harder, and when it's time to try something else? Banging our head against a wall (or a kitchen cabinet) is one good indicator. The "problem" could be a difficult task, a challenging relationship, or an unjust social structure. When our efforts produce nothing but frustration, it's time to step back, question our approach, and seek wisdom from beyond our own narrow viewpoint. One thing is for sure: Doing the wrong thing more vigorously will never yield the right results.

Is there something you've been trying to do that's just not working? In prayer, imagine yourself "trying harder," with all that entails. Notice your feelings. Then imagine what it would be like to let go, to seek counsel, to join effort with others, or to find another path. Notice your feelings again. In which option can you sense the encouragement of God?

PART III

EMBRACING

Through birth and death, in this world or in others, wherever You lead me, it is You, the same, the one Companion of my endless life, who links my heart with bonds of joy to the unfamiliar.

—Rabindranath Tagore

C an you remember your first crush?

Mine was in kindergarten. John sat in front of me, a polite little boy with a friendly smile. One day—spontaneously and inexplicably—I pulled his chair away as he was about to sit down. I don't know if the attraction was mutual, but that certainly wasn't the best way to find out.

The question of whether we are loved, by whom and how well, consumes a tremendous amount of brain space from our earliest days.

As a noun, love is something we can find, or lose, or be in. It can be true or false, with many other nouns masquerading as the real thing: infatuation, possessiveness, dependency, control, or pity, to name just a few of the infinite imposters.

As a verb, love is something we practice, yet practice never makes perfect; there are so many ways for people to disappoint each other. And yet, we keep trying. Love is, after all, what is called for in most circumstances. Once the false varieties have been spotted and rejected, asking "What is the loving thing to do here?" will usually point us in the direction of a good decision.

Though called to love universally, we find our greatest consolation in people who know us by heart—those who recognize our gifts, honor our desires, encourage our growth, and hold harmless our foibles. Some of these dear ones have been with us from the very beginning, yet newcomers are capable of surprising intimacy. I am often moved by how late in life a soul friend can appear. *"It is You, the same, the one Companion of my endless life . . ."*

The stories in this section explore different ways of living lovingly: through a brief encounter, within evolving relationships, between old friends. (There's nothing about romance here, however, because that's not something everyone finds.)

When it comes to love, we are all lifelong learners—or can be, if we let ourselves be taught. Rooted in God's abiding friendship, a world of possible love is ours, each revealing a glimpse of the one Companion's face.

CHAPTER 15

Finding God in a Brown Satin Sheath

Let everyone be quick to listen, slow to speak, slow to anger.

—James 1:19

T he dress caught my eye as it waved in the breeze of a summer garage sale. It was a chocolatey jacquard satin sheath, ankle-length, with an Asian collar. A size two, it would never fit me, but I knew it would look stunning on my cousin Susan, complementing her brown eyes and accenting her willowy figure. I gladly handed over seven dollars and drove straight to her house.

Jumping out of the car, I ran inside, eager to show Susan my beautiful find. I couldn't wait to see it on her! She greeted me with delight, as always, but I absolutely could not get her to pay any attention to the dress. She might have tossed off a halfhearted "That's nice," but she clearly was not as captivated by it as I was, and she definitely wasn't trying it on. Susan's kids were young; it was a typical chaotic Saturday. No amount of effervescence on my part could get a fancy dress to register on her radar screen. A week or two later, I spotted it in a heap on her closet floor.

I'm embarrassed to say that I nursed this grudge for several years. The memory of standing awkwardly in Susan's hallway holding my unappreciated gift joined a litany of other perceived slights. There was the time she returned a novel I had begged her to read; when asked what she thought of a key scene, she confessed that she had only skimmed my underlining. There was the Friday night we arrived at the shore for a getaway just as my all-time favorite *Star Trek* rerun was starting. Susan agreed to watch it, which turned out to mean "tolerated having it on in the background while unpacking." Less jarring but more frequent were the phone calls during which her periodic silences and vague responses revealed that she was also catching up on taped episodes of *Guiding Light*.

In other words, Susan was human. Her death from a brain tumor at age forty-six did not retroactively canonize her every earthly moment. What it did do was give me ample time to reconsider my own role in remembered offenses. What was I not mindful of at the time? I seem to recall that, on the day of the dress incident, Susan's mother (ever-vigilant about germs) was on her way over. Might Susan have feared being caught holding—or, heaven forbid, *wearing*—a musty secondhand dress of unknown origin? On that Friday night at the shore, did I consider how much Susan enjoyed the ritual of unpacking in a new place? Did I ever stop to think how little time she had to read novels, or what consolation she derived from stolen moments with her soap opera after the kids went to bed? More importantly—and this really stings—what could Susan not get *me* to be excited about?

My cousin was a gift from God, obviously more precious than the most fabulous garage-sale find. Did I ever disregard her, like she disregarded that dress? Of course I did—because I'm human, too.

On balance, we cherished each other far more than we let each other down. If memories of missed opportunities can help me tend my present loves more carefully, that will be just one of Susan's many enduring gifts to me.

What grudges or resentments are you holding toward someone you love? Remember that your time with them is finite. How can you forgive their slights and 'fess up to your own more freely?

CHAPTER 16

Finding God in a Juicy Peach

See, now is the acceptable time; see, now is the day of salvation!

—2 Corinthians 6:2

I t was peach season at the Jersey shore. The farm stand on the way to Cape May displayed bountiful baskets right out front—a most effective marketing strategy. We bought a half-bushel, noting that the peaches were still a bit firm and thinking we'd have fruit to enjoy for the whole vacation week. They ripened overnight, which is how we found ourselves standing over the kitchen sink, each devouring a juicy, delicious, perfect peach, and eyeing the rest of the basket with alarm. Now what?

We could have put them into the refrigerator, or baked a cobbler, or made smoothies (ooh, or daiquiris), and they'd have been tasty in all those forms. But they never would be as good as they were right that very minute, dripping warm juice down our chins into the sink.

The peach dilemma—admittedly minor—demonstrates the limitations of my lifelong commitment to delayed gratification. As a child, I was always the one hoarding Easter candy on Memorial Day, and even as an adult I often defer the delightful. Sometimes this approach is grounded in self-control learned at my mother's knee: homework before *Batman*, veggies before dessert. Other times, however, it seems rooted in fear—the old scarcity principle—as though somehow there would be no chocolate left in the world when my foil-wrapped bunnies ran out.

I enjoyed another peach on the spot, but *carpe diem* was not finished with me. That afternoon, I stood at the edge of the surf and watched my friends Jeff and Deb frolic in the ocean while I navigated my usual tension between longing to be in the water and dreading the waves. (Traditionally, I vacillate in the shallows all week before braving it on the last day of vacation, immediately regretting not having taken the plunge earlier.) Suddenly, Jeff raced out of the water, took my hand, and escorted me past the alarming breakers to the sublime rollers beyond, where we floated with ease for almost an hour. It was the longest I'd ever been in the water without being able to touch bottom, and it was pure bliss! The ocean had been beckoning all along, like a basket of ripe peaches. The only sensible course was to dive in.

This experience was especially poignant because Jeff is battling early-onset Alzheimer's. My brilliant and funny friend is still both those things, but the creeping fog is visible. He's in a clinical trial, which may slow the progression and buy him time. But time is not infinite, and the disease is making it clear: To postpone enjoying one another's company is to waste the gift. Like yesterday's ocean or an overripe peach, it's not coming back.

Of course, this is true for all our loves and friendships; we are always running out of time. We just don't acknowledge it most days, because we need to go to work, and cut the grass, and do the wash, and pay the bills. Duty calls; delight can wait. However, neither work, nor grass, nor wash, nor bills negate The Lesson of the Peaches: When life hands me something precious, I want to let myself enjoy it in the measure it deserves.

What gratification do you routinely defer? Is it in the service of something better, or simply a squandered opportunity? What might you resolve to enjoy more fully in the moment, delighting in God's gift?

CHAPTER 17

Finding God in the Chemistry Lab

This is my commandment, that you love one another as I have loved you.

—John 15:12

I had never cut class before. Technically, I wasn't cutting *class*; I was hiding in the lavatory, trying to recover from a crying jag on my way to *lunch*. Nevertheless, in my Catholic, all-girls, nun-run high school, being anyplace other than where you were supposed to be was a dangerous business.

A perfect storm of woe had descended on me. The next day was the first anniversary of my grandfather's death in a terrible accident, and my Algebra II teacher had just returned a test with a big "77" on the front. It was official: My fall semester math grade would not be high enough for Mom to let me try out for the spring musical. *Could this day get any worse?*

As I struggled to return my face to its normal color with a cool, wet paper towel, suddenly I found myself caught in the icy stare of Sister Maureen Michael, the gaunt, unsmiling chemistry teacher. *Where had she come from?* More importantly, *Why couldn't it have been a teacher who knew me?*

"Come this way," she said, and marched down the hall to an empty chem lab with me in mute, miserable tow. Unaccustomed to reprimand, I wondered if I might actually pass out. Then something unexpected happened.

Once in her lab, Sister Michael's face softened. Her eyes grew sympathetic, and she asked, "What's wrong, dear?"

This unexpected kindness unhinged me. It all came pouring out: my grandfather's anniversary, the bad grade, the dashed plans. I wept through the whole story, uncertain what was going to happen next.

"I don't think you need to go to the cafeteria if you don't want to," Sister said thoughtfully. "I'm sure you have homework to do. You're welcome to stay here until the bell rings." And that is exactly what I did; for the rest of the period, I read a book while Sister Michael graded papers. She didn't effuse; she didn't advise. She just gave me what I needed: a safe place to collect myself.

Decades later, I gave a talk on the very stage where I had indeed not performed in the spring musical. I told the students about my crying jag and Sister's kindhearted rescue. Afterwards, a teacher who had been there forever told me something I had not known at the time: That year, Sister Michael had been fighting a losing battle with cancer. Throughout treatment, she had taught her classes, monitored the halls, and observed her girls. Seeing past the looming specter of her terminal illness, she had looked with compassion on my transient grief, and offered comfort from what must have been a limited store.

That brief encounter was a profound experience of what spiritual writers call "disinterested love." Disinterested is not the same as *un*interested; indeed, it is quite the opposite: passionate interest in another person, in the absence of any *self*-interest.

As a campus minister, educator, and human being, I have had countless opportunities to "pay forward" the disinterested love I received in my moment of adolescent despair. Some I've caught, and some I've missed, but I know this: Each new day offers a new chance to practice.

Spend some time with the idea of disinterested love—care that is free of self-interest. Do you believe it is rare or common in the world today? When have you received or given that kind of love?

CHAPTER 18

Finding God in Book Money

Well done, *good and faithful servant.*

—Matthew 25:23

L iz had no idea how she was going to pay for college. She'd been working at a grocery store since she was fifteen, but her modest earnings were pocket change compared to the cost of tuition. She couldn't take out a loan because no relative was in a position to co-sign. Decision day was approaching. She was almost out of time, and definitely out of options.

Suddenly, a name popped into her head: Mr. Minier, the grocery store owner. Running his family business and putting three kids through college, he seemed more financially stable than anyone she knew. Though awash in embarrassment for both her poverty and her failure to come up with a better plan, Liz gathered her courage, walked into her boss's office, and made the impossible ask: Could he co-sign her loan?

Retelling the story years later, Liz shook her head at her own naïveté, chagrined by the magnitude of her completely unrealistic request. Running a family business with three kids in college was a high-wire juggling act, not financial stability. Mr. Minier had to say no—but he didn't stop at no. Instead, he pulled out his checkbook, gave Liz $500 for books, and assured her that she could come back to him every semester for book money.

Inspired by her boss's confidence in her ability to persevere, Liz found a way. She spent a year in community college, working thirty-five hours a week as night manager at Minier's and establishing a credit score that enabled her to sign for her own loan and transfer to a state university. It took ten semesters, but the grocer came through with book money every time.

After commencement, Liz accepted a temporary position in a college financial aid office where—five years, one graduate degree, and four promotions later—she became the director of the department. Knowing in her bones the terror of not having a clue how to afford a desperately wanted education, Liz dedicated herself to identifying every dollar to which her students were entitled, while never encouraging them to take on more debt than they could afford. Quietly, she went the extra mile over and over again: finding space in the residence halls when commuter students were rendered homeless; arranging gas and grocery cards for those whose path to graduation was blocked by an unexpected need.

She never forgot the kindness of her former boss. He had believed in her and had put his faith into action. Liz says that by investing in her potential, Mr. Minier inspired her to invest in herself, as she put every possible effort into succeeding in school. More importantly, his generous reaction to her embarrassing request set the standard for the type of person she now strives to be. Her career in financial aid has multiplied that investment exponentially.

"I believe in you." It's one of the most loving things we can say to a person—especially when those words are accompanied by practical action. It doesn't have to involve a checkbook. When we penetrate someone's fog of self-doubt and fix our gaze on their potential, for that moment we are helping them to see themselves through God's eyes. It's a tremendous gift, one which may cost us nothing—or everything. Will we take the risk?

Who has invested in your potential over the years? Is there someone you know who is struggling with self-doubt now? How can you demonstrate your confidence in them?

CHAPTER 19

Finding God in Good Questions

And he said to them, "What are you discussing with each other while you walk along?"

—Luke 24:17

I was in the car with my brother Stephen's new boyfriend, John; it was our first time alone together. Near the beginning of our two-hour drive, John posed a little icebreaker: "How is your having a partner with cancer different from having had parents with cancer?" (Apparently, softball questions were not John's forte.)

I had no simple answer. My parents' cancers had been caught late and advanced quickly; Porter's had been detected early enough to be kept at bay. The diagnoses were different, but what *in me* was new this time? The long, exploring conversation got us halfway to Baltimore.

John's question stayed with me because it was only the first of his many thought-provoking queries. A few weeks later, as we were about to see each other again, I began thinking what I might ask him. I pondered what I knew about John already. What was I curious about, that a good question could help illuminate? What backstory, essential to his self-understanding, could I draw out with a well-framed inquiry? He had raised the conversational bar, and I was determined to meet him there.

Now that John's been in my life long enough to go from brother's-new-boyfriend to brother-in-law, our frequent chats flow more spontaneously, but I remain moved by that initial thoughtful question. What I experienced from John was a particular form of care. *I've been thinking about you*, a good question says. *I see you, and I want to know you more deeply.* What a gift. It is so easy to exchange pleasantries or swap monologues, blathering on about ourselves and leaving the people around us feeling lonely at best, invisible at worst. The careful question opens a merciful space for genuine encounter—especially when careful listening follows.

There is an art to asking good questions (not to be confused with the prying, invasive sort, which no one needs). Skilled therapists and spiritual directors practice this art. Rather than dispensing answers like prescriptions, they help us follow Rilke's advice in *Letters to a Young Poet:* "Be patient toward all that is unsolved in your heart and try to love the questions themselves . . ." Questions worth loving unlock a treasure chest of memory and meaning.

Scripture is full of such questions. In Genesis, after the incident with the fruit, God asks Adam and Eve, "Where are you?" and "Who told you that you were naked?" In Mark, Jesus asks the blind beggar, Bartimaeus, "What do you want me to do for you?" In Luke, the risen Savior asks his despondent disciples, "What are you discussing with each other while you walk along?" In each story, gracious questions help the hearers bring their own truth to light. That is something we can do for our own conversation partners now.

Good questions are hospitable. With families spread across the country, an unprecedented number of Americans living alone, and "social distancing" a matter of public health, such hospitality is desperately needed today. Hospitable questions brew a pot of tea, put out a plate of scones, pull up a chair at our hearth, and invite people to make themselves at home.

How divine!

Imagine God pulling up a chair beside you, companionably offering a good question. What would God ask? How would you respond? On the other hand, what question could you ask a friend or loved one that would invite them to speak their own truth?

CHAPTER 20

Finding God Unleashed

Do not quench the Spirit.

—1 Thessalonians 5:19

The dog I love most in the world just turned seven. Lazarus is an aptly named rescue: eighty pounds of energy and affection, dignified except when he's being silly. He is my brother's housemate (or so I assume he regards himself, not feeling *owned* by anyone). Being seven makes Laz a firmly middle-aged dog, as I have been for some time a firmly middle-aged woman. We're both showing our gray, feeling creaky in the joints, and inclined to couch naps after long walks. He is excellent company.

On a summer trip to Maine, we took Laz to a nature preserve and set off down a trail into the woods. I brought up the rear, picking my way cautiously with a hiking pole for balance. He strained at the leash, whistling like a teakettle with frenzied impatience. So much to see! So much to smell! Hurry up, people!

The preserve had only a few cars in the parking lot, and no one in sight or earshot. The posted rules said that dogs must be "leashed or under voice control." Laz is a good boy. Stephen unclipped the lead.

He bounded away from us, all muscle and joy. At the sound of his name, Laz whirled and returned, surefooted and exalting. He continued foraging ahead and doubling back until we followed a sign marked "Vista" to some big rocks above the Sheepscot River. Perhaps not understanding that vista meant *view*, Laz leaped without hesitation—and disappeared under the water. Momentarily surprised by its depth, he popped up and swam strongly to shore, shaking off before running back in after a thrown stick. It was a fabulous afternoon.

Over the next few days, I found myself savoring those memories of Laz, and they stirred something in me. He was so *free*, so glad in his body, as I so often am not. As an introvert of Irish descent, I know I am stiff in more than just my joints. Like Martha in Luke's Gospel (sister of Lazarus—how about that), I work the perimeter of a party rather than plop myself down in the center of the fun. When worship turns exuberant at my church, I can feel the rigor mortis setting in, as I simultaneously judge and envy those who can give over their whole body to praise.

Replaying those mental images of Laz, I felt a yearning to move more freely, less self-consciously in this world. What would it be like to follow my joy and see where it takes me, like Laz disappearing into the trees? What experience might I dive into, heedless of the water's depth? Conversely, to what fears or assumptions have I tethered my own lead, discouraging the exploration of intriguing paths beyond midlife?

I am drawn to the energy I experienced in Laz unleashed, and I believe that there is something of God's desire for me in there as well. I need to sit with that desire, to notice when I'm following it—and when I'm not.

In her poignant book *Dog Songs*, Mary Oliver imagines a conversation with a pup who claims to know nothing of prayer. "Every time you wake up and love your life and the world, you're praying, my dear boy. I'm sure of it," she insists. Waking up, loving my life, loving the world: that's a good place to start.

Where are you on the reserved-to-exuberant spectrum? When do you hold yourself back, in opposition to your own deep desires? In prayer, imagine yourself unleashed. What would you do?

CHAPTER 21

Finding God in Sugar-Covered Strawberries

Love never ends.

—I Corinthians 13:8

W hen I was little, my grandmother taught me how to eat a strawberry: after removing the leaves, spear berry with fork, plunge directly into open sugar bowl, pop in mouth, repeat. (It took me years to realize I shouldn't eat them that way in public.)

Even without the added sugar, my grandmother brought sweetness to so many of my early memories. As the oldest grandchild, I enjoyed the youngest version of her: the grandmother who zipped around town in a Chevy Vega (hot orange, no less), who was always game for a boardwalk roller coaster, and who kept her kitchen stocked with Pepperidge Farm cookies and strawberries ripe for the bowl.

It wasn't that she'd never known sorrow. In fact, Gram had seen more than her share. Her baby brother perished in World War II and her only son died in his crib. In her fifties, she lost her mother to breast cancer and her husband to cardiac arrest within six weeks of each other. Yet, somehow, those losses didn't leave a shadow—at least, not one her grandchildren could see. Even after a broken hip at age seventy rendered her fragile, she remained classy, funny, and generous. ("Now, get something you really want," she always said when taking someone out to dinner; she didn't want us ordering pizza instead of prime rib just to save her a few pennies.)

The shadow didn't appear until she turned eighty, when Alzheimer's began to wage its insidious campaign against her personality. She suffered its assault for seventeen years, dying at age ninety-seven in my aunt and uncle's home, where she'd lived since it became clear she could no longer be alone.

Hers was a fate most of us dread, yet what strikes me now is how much good Gram enkindled, even then. During those awful years, her illness became a hub around which many lives revolved, as relatives rallied to provide company and care. For her funeral service, we selected the First Corinthians reading about love because so many of us had become more patient and kind, less self-interested and record-of-wrong-keeping for having been part of the family during Gram's final years. She lived those virtues until the Alzheimer's took her volition, at which point she inspired them. The care that flowed back to her was a return of the tide, a response of love to one who had been so steadfast.

Gram's impact in her decline was not limited to immediate family. One summer during our shore vacation, she was in a phase where she would read aloud anything put in front of her—from fine literature to toothpaste ads—so my mother had packed a book of daily meditations by one of Gram's favorite saints, Francis de Sales. I spent many afternoons cross-stitching on the couch while she read those beautiful words (and page numbers, and running headers) in her oddly monotone voice. They sank in.

By the end of the two weeks, I had designed a plan for college students to use that book—and, subsequently, others in the series—in a monthlong spirituality program that eventually won a national campus ministry award. Each time we ran the program, I made sure my students knew it had been inspired by my grandmother, Mary Florence Reilly: an octogenarian with Alzheimer's whom God was still using to sweeten everyday life.

Many of us have a great fear of outliving our "usefulness," but loving my grandmother taught me to measure life's goodness differently. Whom do you cherish, just for who they are? Bask in imagining being so cherished yourself.

PART IV

RELEASING

When one knows You, then alien there is none, then no door is shut.
O grant me my prayer that I may never lose the bliss of the touch of the one in the play of the many.

—Rabindranath Tagore

L ife is filled with loss. We lose loved ones to geography, estrangement, and death. We bury pets and move away from places we were happy. Our bodies let us down, gradually or dramatically. Dreams die—sometimes hard—and even a dream fulfilled means abandoning other lovely possibilities. Every time we turn around, it seems, we're being challenged to sacrifice something we'd rather keep.

"Let go and let God!" These words are a source of deep consolation to some, mystifying aggravation to others. The first time I heard the expression, I thought it was novel and clever. Like most pious platitudes, however, it lost its appeal over time. It's not that I don't believe in releasing my white-knuckled grip on things and summoning a little trust in my Maker; on the contrary, I know that's usually the right thing to do. I also know it's rarely as easy as the five-word slogan implies.

It is agonizing to let go of people, places, and roles that we love—including our beloved illusion of control. The stories in this section circle around the human impulse to hold on to things as they are—even when we are in pain—versus the invitation to release ourselves and follow God into an unknown future. Whether we are trapped by grief or anxiety, relentless obsession or false obligation, the clarion call sounds: Let it go. Trust what's next.

Reading Tagore's prayer, I find it fascinating that there is just one thing he does not want to lose: *the bliss of the touch of the one in the play of the many*—in other words, the joy of sensing

God's familiar presence in surprising places. He knows what we so often forget: It's the divine spark that makes the people and things we love lovable, and that spark does not disappear when they do. God's love abides, even when disguised. Only one question remains: Will we let ourselves risk loving again?

CHAPTER 22

Finding God in Tears

My tears have been my food day and night,
while people say to me continually, "Where is your God?"

—Psalm 42:3

Hannah could not stop crying. She had come on retreat to find some peace, but all the silence had created was more space for her grief to unfurl itself. Without the distraction of intense work or casual conversation, Hannah's mind was free to roam the nooks and crannies of her memories, probing for open wounds.

In the space of just a few months, she had suffered a painful diminishment in her body and the violent death of a dear friend. Either would have been hard to bear; together, they were threatening to undo her. These twin blows were compounded by her need to maintain the appearance of resilience; people were so upset by what had happened to her that she often found herself consoling *them*. This relentless coping was threatening to become a traumatic experience of its own. And yet, she kept on keeping on—because that's what she always did.

People used many adjectives to describe Hannah—valiant, heroic, brave, strong—but she didn't feel like any of those things. She felt only the crushing awareness of life being consumed, whether in small bites—as with her body—or swallowed whole—as with her friend. She might have been recovering physically, but emotionally, she was shellacked with grief.

Though she didn't feel particularly brave or strong, Hannah did one of the strongest and bravest things possible on that retreat: She took her devastation to prayer. In her imagination, she gathered the rubble of her life and constructed a brick structure around herself. Its purpose was to protect her from more pain, but with each layer stacked and sealed, she felt herself increasingly cut off from everyone who loved her. Eventually, she bricked in the space overhead, shutting out even the sunlight. In the dark little prison she had built for herself, Hannah began to keen.

Gradually, her prayer shifted. Instead of writing a script, it began to seem as though she were watching a movie. She noticed that the dried mud between the bricks was beginning to soften and melt, dripping down around her. From inside the shelter, Hannah heard the sound of someone else weeping, and realized that the salty water dissolving her protective structure was actually tears, falling on the roof from the outside.

Who could have wept more than she? The question caught her breath. As the bricks above loosened and fell, she saw Jesus bent over her, sobbing brokenhearted tears for her pain and her isolation. Even though Hannah did not think she'd been blaming God for what had happened, this outpouring of divine compassion was astonishing. Knowing herself so powerfully understood and accompanied, Hannah sensed her spirit turning the slightest of corners.

Who could have wept more than she? Who could have wept more than you, or me, at our lowest? Some seek comfort in the idea of a God who makes everything happen for a reason—one whose good if unfathomable motive underlies even the most horrifying tragedy. This conviction, however, risks keeping God at arm's length. To be embraced by a God who weeps opens the door to a more intimate relationship with the One who knows us, who suffers with us, and who continuously loves us into life.

Is there a sorrow you have carried too long? (If you are truly anguished and stuck, have you sought therapy or spiritual direction?) Try bringing it to prayer—from a very safe space. Can you let yourself feel God's companioning sorrow? What happens?

CHAPTER 23

Finding God in the Next Generation

It is more blessed to give than to receive.

—Acts 20:35

Mary Ellen had raised six children on her own. A fiercely independent English professor with an equally fierce intellect, she'd spent decades helping with homework, attending parent-teacher conferences, bandaging scraped knees, sitting in emergency rooms, putting food on the table, and generally keeping the family ship afloat. Sacrificing much of her life for her children, she embodied the eucharistic quality of motherhood: This is my body; this is my blood. Now, one of her daughters was in trouble, and Mary Ellen couldn't help.

Caitlyn lived alone, in Florida—a thousand miles away. She was gravely ill, but the operation she needed had just been postponed because preoperative testing had revealed a cancer even more urgently in need of surgery. Mary Ellen wanted nothing more than to race to the airport, hop on a plane, and fly to her daughter's aid. But she had just turned eighty, had a distressing medical affliction of her own, and was awaiting surgery to repair a botched hip replacement. Racing, hopping, and flying were all out of the question; she was more likely to become the emergency than assuage it. This was a mother's nightmare.

Then, her son Brad called. He was due some vacation time at work, and his wife could spare him for a while. What if he flew to Florida for the surgery and stayed with his sister through the worst of her recovery?

Brad's offer was practically vertigo-inducing. Mary Ellen was so accustomed to being the conductor of this orchestra; it felt surreal that the kids might work it out without her. At first, she raged against her own disability; she wanted to be the one at the bedside! Then she realized something. Perhaps *being there* was not the best gift she could give her children. Since she would not live forever, would not—she prayed—outlive them all, maybe a better gift would be the experience of relying on one other. How touching for Caitlyn, to have her brother drop everything and come take care of her. How meaningful for Brad, to know what he may only have hoped—that he was the sort of person who would do such a thing.

"It is more blessed to give than to receive," Scripture says. It also just feels better. Who among us would not rather be on the giving end of charity? It is lovely to be lauded for one's generosity, or even to do some bit of anonymous good and watch the outcome with quiet satisfaction. It is much harder to look humble and grateful while someone else meets the need. And yet, if we are forever playing the starring role of helper, what becomes of the understudy? If we never pass the ball, who else can take the shot?

Of course, often it's not a zero-sum game; two people can be generous without either diminishing the other. But every once in a while, when we are tempted to raise our hand *again*, it might be worth pausing to notice if there is someone else who would shine—if only they could get out from behind our shadow.

It is more blessed to give than to receive, but there's a sneaky corollary: It may be even more blessed to let someone else have the blessing.

What responsibility do you take pride in having on your shoulders? What have you long received affirmation for doing? Look around. Is there someone else who might like to try? Can you be generous and let them?

CHAPTER 24

Finding God in a Toy Truck

And this is my prayer, that your love may overflow more and more with knowledge
and full insight to help you determine what is best.

—Philippians 1:9–10

The present that had thrilled my little brother the day before was making him miserable already. Someone had given Stephen a toy truck with a "pull-back" mechanism that allowed him to roll the vehicle backwards along the floor a few feet and then release it for a run of several yards. We should have read the operating instructions more carefully, as this toy was meant to be used on hard surfaces only. Stephen had been playing with it in the kitchen and on the porch, but soon the living room rug beckoned. It was a German-shepherd-colored shag, chosen by our parents to camouflage both paw prints and shedding. The truck made just a couple passes before it stopped working altogether. Whether clogged by dog fur or carpet fibers, that gizmo was kaput.

This mishap faded from memory until my senior year of college, when I developed a crush on a guy who was way too cool for me (in a long-haired, tie-dyed, guitar-group kind of way).

After sharing a couple theology classes, Joe and I had started volunteering together with a street outreach program on Sunday nights, hitting the campus Gino's for fried chicken afterward. It was a swell camaraderie, but I was firmly in the friend zone.

One night, I decided to take it to prayer. What was God's desire for this relationship in my life? I was not really expecting an answer, but the image of that little truck popped into my mind at once. It occurred to me that Stephen could have enjoyed his toy until he outgrew it, if only we'd followed the instructions. Suddenly, I understood that I had a choice: I could appreciate my time with Joe straight through to graduation, or I could try to push the friendship somewhere else and wreck it. For the rest of the year, I was able to delight in those Sunday-night outings without angling or pining for more. I didn't seal off my heart so Joe wouldn't break it; I genuinely let go of the romance I thought I wanted.

This may have been my first experience of swiftly answered prayer, which is probably why I remember it so clearly. Just as Jesus did with all those parables about sheep and coins and vineyards, God used the ordinary stuff of my life—a little plastic truck—to teach me what I hadn't been able to learn any other way.

Joe and I lost touch after graduation, but our brief friendship bore fruit, as Scripture says, a hundredfold. Over our weekly chicken and biscuits, Joe shared his passion for social justice, instilled by a favorite high school teacher. That teacher went on to run the house of hospitality in Richmond where I wound up living and working in community the following year. There I met Jeff, who married my cousin Susan. They had two children; their granddaughter Sookie is now approaching the age Stephen was when that toy truck ground to a halt.

Joe's friendship was a gift from God. I'm so glad I read the "operating instructions" in time!

Is there a relationship in your life that is not "working"? It doesn't have to be a romance; you could be a stepparent, a supervisor, even a neighbor. Hold it in prayer and see if any divine blueprints begin to be revealed.

CHAPTER 25

Finding God in Goodbyes

Lord, if it is you, command me to come to you on the water.

—Matthew 14:28

A fter nearly ten years in my first campus ministry position, I reached a heart-wrenching insight during my summer retreat: It was time to look for a new job. My reluctance might sound ridiculous; I know the average worker changes jobs in half that time. But, after a rocky start, I had come to love the place. Working there felt like being in the middle of a three-generation family. Our secretary and handyman were my parents' age, while a gaggle of kids (better known as young adults) enlivened the building at all hours, growing in faith as they found comfort in our home away from home. (As one student said, "You're like my mom, only you're not yelling at me.") Telling them I wanted to leave was going to feel personal.

And yet, though our campus ministry center was a wonderful world, it was both small and all-consuming. During the academic year, we were open until ten o'clock five nights a week, which had kept me from most ordinary social interaction for almost a decade. Having little opportunity to meet people my own age, I was starting to feel a yearning for what I called "more life in my life." In my journal, I wrote, "If I drop dead of sleep deprivation at age 53 after working here for 25 years, will I believe I spent those years wisely? Well, I'm 40% of the way there already!"

It was a strange experience, feeling called away from something I cherished. At a lake near the retreat house, I found myself praying with the Scripture passage where Saint Peter walks on water. The story goes like this: The apostles were out in their boat in the wee hours when they saw a figure walking toward them. Were they seeing things, or was it Jesus?

"Lord," said Peter (always impulsive), "if it is you, command me to come to you on the water." Why on earth would Peter imagine he could walk on water? Nevertheless, at Jesus' invitation, Peter left his familiar boat and did the unthinkable, starting to sink only when he got distracted by the ferocity of the wind.

Again, in my journal I wrote, "Beloved, if you want me somewhere else, just tell me. If I fix my gaze on you and keep it there, all will be well. Now, is it really you? If so, tell me to come!"

I went home, had the hard conversations, and buffed up my résumé.

The following summer, I became the director of campus ministry at a Catholic university, where I served for fifteen years, until another wave of desire drew me into the uncharted waters of a freelance existence.

Does it sound odd to talk about "waves of desire" in a religious context? Many of us were taught to be suspicious of our own desires. In Ignatian spirituality, however, we believe it is God who plants in us the deepest longings of our hearts (not to be confused with lesser wants, which could be from our own minds or even the suggestion of an evil spirit).

That is why it is so important that we carve out time for silence. Letting the buzz of passing fancies and the thrum of daily life subside, we can listen for the deep, steady beat of longing that reveals God's desire in us.

If you are feeling restless, prayerfully try to imagine what the life you long for might look like. Be as specific as possible. In these fantasies, can you notice something of God's desire for your fullness of life? What might you do about that?

CHAPTER 26

Finding God in a Pod of Dolphins

I believe that I shall see the goodness of the LORD in the land of the living.

—Psalm 27:13

I stood at the water's edge with my back to the beach, tears streaming down my face. How could my mother be gone? This time last year, she'd been a month into treatment, and I had come here to the shore for two nights' respite between doctors' appointments. Praying on the balcony, I'd seen a hummingbird—a sign, for me, of God's reassuring presence. Then the cascade of organ failures had begun. Surgeons and oncologists marshaled increasingly painful interventions, all for naught. Eleven weeks to the day from Mom's diagnosis, we stood by her casket.

Being at the shore with extended family highlighted my mother's absence painfully, but that wasn't what had gotten me just then. Instead, I was lost in memories of those awful last weeks of her life. Mom's primary care physician had gently raised the question of hospice, but the other doctors weren't ready to sound a retreat from the battleground of her body. As the daughter, I was the one who had stayed by Mom's bedside through intimate procedures, leaving me with memories I couldn't scour from my brain; the callousness of one thoracic surgeon haunts me still. The woman I loved so much had suffered so terribly. It had been my job to protect her, and I had failed.

My eyes were blurred with tears, but the sound of *oohs* and *aahs* made me blink them away to see what the other beachgoers had noticed. In the ocean, just a handful of yards from shore, dolphins were frolicking. This wasn't the steady progression of a pod traveling by, as we often saw; this was *play*. They leaped and splashed, twisted and spun in the air, and smacked the water with their tails on their way back down. They appeared awash in delight.

That's what it's like for me now.

The thought came unbidden, in my mother's voice. It hit me that Mom was no longer trapped in her failing body, enduring dreadful procedures. I was the one stuck doing battle reenactments—questioning every decision, replaying torturous memories until my imaginary videotape was worn thin. Mom had suffered, yes; those weeks had been excruciating. But they were over; no one could hurt her anymore. She was free.

"He is not here," angels told the women that first Easter morning. Jesus wasn't in the empty tomb, and Mom wasn't in the hospital room. If I wanted to be where she was, I had to quit staring at where she'd been.

I can't say it happened all at once, but I have finally stopped hitting REPLAY. Now, I see Mom's face in the mirror as my age approaches her own, and hear her voice whenever someone channels her wit. I find her in the joyful memories I share with the family she adored, and in the delight she would have felt in the children who arrived after she left. I sit at her feet every time I draw on her practical wisdom, and laugh with her every time I exclaim, "Mom was right!"

"Why do you look for the living among the dead?" the angels asked. Our loved ones live; this I believe. We have to seek them among the living.

What does it mean for you to seek a deceased loved one among the living? Call someone to mind in prayer. Where and how are they alive in you, and in the world and people around you?

CHAPTER 27

Finding God in a Broken Glass

And remember, I am with you always, to the end of the age.

—Matthew 28:20

I flipped on the bathroom light in dismay, fighting to keep my emotions at bay as I stared at the broken glass in the sink. "It's just a thing," I said aloud, to no one, repeating it like a mantra as I stoically placed the fragments in a brown paper bag. Nevertheless, my rising panic suggested that this glass was way more than "just a thing."

Seven years after my mother died, my father followed. When my brother and I cleaned out their house to sell it, I didn't have room for much. I kept my mother's rocking chair, my father's mantel clock, my grandfather's cookie press, and a few other mementos—including one brightly colored pint glass. I don't remember when my parents got it, only that it had become "my" glass whenever I visited home. I couldn't bear to send it to a thrift store, so I brought it to my house. And then I broke it.

It was just a thing—a lifeless object. Why was I feeling panic?

Naturally, I was sad; the glass was a tangible reminder of happier times. Drinking from it brought me back to shooting the breeze with my mother over cold Cokes on a hot afternoon, or carefully pouring a Guinness as my father recounted his latest strategy to keep squirrels out of the bird feeder. The way Mom always reached for it when I arrived made me feel known and cherished. That's a lot of emotional weight to put on one glass; no wonder it shattered. (Truthfully, I had misjudged the distance to the bathroom faucet in the dark, though the symbolic pressure didn't help.) But, again, why panic?

I realize now that what I feared was not sadness, but the return of *grief*—sharp and unexpected as an overlooked shard of glass. Dad had been gone for almost a year, Mom for more than eight, and even the wretched house clean-out was nine months behind us. I was no longer dwelling in my sorrow; I was living my life, just getting an ordinary drink of water before bed. Having survived the ocean of grief, I did not want to be pulled back under by a rogue wave in one klutzy move. That's what the panic was about: I was afraid of drowning.

I would love to tell you that I turned to prayer that night, but I did not. Instead of trusting God to hold my hand through the fear, I simply turned on National Public Radio and tried to lose myself in the news of the world until I fell asleep.

What I wish I had realized is that drowning was not my only option. Towering waves of emotion come, but they also go. In this case, the pain of losing "just a thing" was all caught up in memories of love and joy. That's the comforting shore I might have reached if I'd had the courage to ride out the feeling, like I would have ridden a wave as a child: not cowering before it, but moving with it . . . not being pummeled by grief, but letting it carry me home.

Is there a loss that threatens to overwhelm you, even from a distance of time? (Have you spoken with a dear friend or relative about it? What about a therapist or spiritual guide?) When you are in a safe place, imagine God taking your hand and promising you not to let go. Allow yourself to move with the grief, instead of fighting to hold it at bay. Where does it carry you?

CHAPTER 28

Finding God at Home (Again)

Those who go out weeping, bearing the seed for sowing,
shall come home with shouts of joy, carrying their sheaves.

—Psalm 126:6

The text from our cousin caught my brother and me completely by surprise: "Just drove by—your parents' house is for sale!"

How could that be? The woman who'd bought it from us five years earlier had gushed about how thrilled she was to find her "forever home." That was the main reason we'd sold it to her, even though she'd been the first person to tour the house. We had been consoled by the fact that the dwelling our family had cherished for thirty-five years would be loved into life again—yet already it was back on the market.

Though I'd been heartbroken to let it go, only my brother had seriously flirted with the idea of trying to hold on to the hundred-year-old, six-bedroom, three-story house. But, at the time of our father's death, Stephen had both a job and a relationship in another state; he was in no position to consider it seriously. However, in the intervening years he'd found the man he would marry—back home in Philadelphia—and had been promoted to a job he could do from anywhere. One day after our cousin's text, my brother called me. "John and I have decided to make an offer."

Christmas morning found us opening presents in the old living room just as we always had: listening to Bing Crosby albums, drinking coffee with Irish cream, and pausing our conversation each time the cuckoo clock did its thing. John's warmhearted parents, Roseanne and Michael, joined us for dinner, and Stephen and I enjoyed a delightful evening with three people we hadn't even *met* yet when we sold the house.

On the phone the next day, Stephen asked, "Were you okay last night? You slipped away for a while. It wouldn't be the first time you'd cried in the bathroom on Christmas!" He was referring to the several Christmas dinners we'd hosted in the house after Mom died, so he was right to ask—yet he couldn't have been more wrong. Standing in the upstairs hallway, surrounded by a potent mixture of things both foreign and familiar, I'd been awash in recollection but by no means wrecked.

In every room, ghostly memories of our mother's final illness, our father's months on hospice, and our disposal of (almost) all their belongings could have overwhelmed the present happiness—but only if I let them. Instead, I was able to allow the sorrowful past and the joyful present to dwell side by side. I discovered that time, while not erasing the grief, had softened it, carving out space to receive this new, astounding goodness. Celebrating Christmas with John and his parents in the old homestead, I realized that God had given us new people to love in the literal place of our loss.

I am a firm believer in this line from the Catholic funeral liturgy: "For your faithful people, Lord, life is changed, not ended." I've come to understand that this can be true not only for the deceased, but for the bereaved.

Life is changed. It is far from ended.

And it may yet be glorious.

Getting the house back was such a shocking turn of events that I really can't say, "Has anything like this ever happened to you?" So instead, I'll ask this: What space has grief carved out in you? In that space, who or what is God inviting you to love?

Abide with Me

Abide with me! Fast falls the eventide,
The darkness deepens—Lord, with me abide!
When other helpers fail, and comforts flee,
Help of the helpless, O abide with me!

Swift to its close ebbs out life's little day;
Earth's joys grow dim, its glories pass away;
Change and decay in all around I see;
O Thou, who changest not, abide with me!

I fear no foe, with Thee at hand to bless;
Ills have no weight, and tears no bitterness;
Where is death's sting? where, grave, Thy victory?
I triumph still, if Thou abide with me.

Hold Thou Thy cross before my closing eyes;
Shine thro' the gloom and point me to the skies;
Heav'n's morning breaks, and earth's vain shadows flee;
In life, in death, O Lord, abide with me!

—Henry Francis Lyte (1793–1847)

Questions for Conversation

I wrote *Finding God Abiding* with the individual reader in mind, but I can also imagine it as a fruitful resource for dialogue between good friends or in faith-sharing groups. Clear-eyed conversation can help us catch a glimpse of what Virginia Woolf called "the spot the size of a shilling at the back of the head which one can never see for oneself."

If you are praying with this book in the company of others, here are additional questions that may give you a glimpse of the back of your head—or the front of your tapestry.

Regarding the four movements:

- *Finding God Abiding* describes four basic movements: awakening to the world around us (Perceiving); discovering and rediscovering our path (Becoming); practicing love in its many forms (Embracing); and grieving the loss of much that we hold dear (Releasing). Which of these movements do you feel you have practiced the most?

- On the other hand, which movement feels most uncomfortable? How might you stretch yourself to practice it more intentionally?

- From whom did you learn how to see, to make your way in the world, to grow in love, or to let things go? How do you feel about the models you were shown? Whose example would you like to follow now?

Within any of the movements:

- Which of the reflections spoke to you the most? Why do you think that was?
- Was there one you found more difficult to connect with? What didn't work for you?
- If your group were to write a series of reflections on this topic, which story from your own life would you contribute?

A God Who Abides:

- Read aloud the Tagore poem at the beginning of the book. Which words or phrases most resonate? What recollections do they evoke?
- If you are a person who prays, how do you address God? Do you have a favorite divine name? What do you think of Tagore's "*one Companion of my endless life*"?
- Can you relate to the weaving imagery? If you've ever done a handicraft with a back side that was a mess even though the front looked presentable, how does that remind you of your own life?

Perceiving:

- They say hindsight is 20/20. Can you share a story from your past that you saw one way at the time, and understand very differently now? Who or what helped you to view it with new eyes?

- So much of the unrest in America today seems to be caused by people's inability to see things from another's perspective. When have you been given the grace of empathetic vision? Whose experience do you wish you could perceive more clearly now?

- Is there a dilemma in your life that you are having trouble seeing your way through? Invite your conversation partner(s) to pose questions that could help you clarify your thinking. (The Quaker clearness committee—a process used to help individuals tap into their own inner wisdom—provides an outstanding model for asking helpful, agenda-free questions.)

Becoming:

- What is the earliest thing you can remember wanting to be when you grew up? Does your life today have any roots in that early desire?

- Can you give an example of a pivot point in your own story where you could have gone one direction or another, to very different outcomes?

- Listen to Charlie King's folk song, "Our Life Is More than Our Work." What do you think is the difference between your life and your work? Your work and your job? What other song might you choose to represent your life's journey?

Embracing:

- Who are the most significant loves in your life? How did your love grow and change over time? What tested it? Made it stronger?
- Who are the soul friends in your life today? Have you known them forever, or discovered them only recently (or somewhere in between)? What do you value most about your connection?
- Share a story of someone you know who loves very well. What makes their way of loving so remarkable? What about them would you like to emulate?

Releasing:

- When have you been challenged to let go of something or someone important to you? How did you handle it?
- How do you deal with accumulated possessions? Do you find it effortless or excruciating to say goodbye to objects connected with memory? Why do you think that is?
- When have you experienced surprising joy in the midst of sorrow—or a burst of sorrow in the midst of joy? How did you hold these "contradictory" emotions?

Tagore says of God, "*You have brought the distant near and have made a brother [or a sister] of the stranger.*" Since God has brought you together with one another for this time of shared reading and reflection, here are a few final questions to shed light on that experience.

Finding God Together:

- What can you perceive more clearly now, as a result of your conversations?
- As people shared stories of turning points in their lives, did you notice any common threads?
- How have group members modeled God's abiding love to you?
- What did you learn from another person about how to let go of hard things?
- Listen together to a recording of the hymn "Abide with Me." As you pray along with the words, notice any feelings moving within you. What can you share?

Scripture Index

All citations are from the *New Revised Standard Version* of the Bible unless otherwise indicated.

Gratitudes

This book is dedicated to my maternal grandmother, Mary Florence Reilly, née McDevitt. In a life filled with too much sorrow, she never lost her faith, and she never lost her sense of humor—two things I pray I will always be able to say about myself.

Gram's frequent encouragement to "get what you really want" is lodged in my imagination. Though she usually meant, "Order the filet mignon, not the vegetable lasagna," her sensitivity to *desire* took root in me. Thanks to her, I've been able to pursue the dream of becoming a "freelance me," which had long been my answer whenever someone asked me—as an adult— what I wanted to be when I grew up.

I got what I really wanted, Gram. Thanks for believing in me.

Also and always worthy of thanks:

- Everyone connected to the Jesuit Center for Spiritual Growth in Wernersville, PA, whose doors are now closed. For thirty-four years, that holy place formed me in the ways of Ignatian spirituality. Though doubly Jesuit-educated, I learned the most inside your cloister walks. Special thanks to Brother Chris Derby, SJ, for making me laugh and hiring me for stuff; to David Gross—now gone to God—for reminding me how unexpectedly a soul friend can appear; and to Susan Bowers, for gently and passionately companioning my spirit for this entire millennium, AMDG.

- My four early readers: Mary Ellen Graham, Ron Knapp, Rob McChesney, SJ, and Diane Zieg. Your keen eyes and unique perspectives were essential to working through challenges and clarifying obscurities. I value each of you for your friendship, honesty, and spiritual wisdom, which far surpass even your excellent writing chops.

- The good folks at Woodhall Press, who welcomed me into their stable on the recommendation of Steve Eisner at When Words Count. It's been a pleasure!

- My wise and witty editor, Peggy Moran. Although I now have an internalized "Peggy voice," you still manage to make my writing better, every time. Thank you for getting me.

- My talented cover designer, Asha Hossain, who did not shrink from the challenge of making this cover "just like the last one, only different." So many people read my words because your artistry draws them to pick up my books; I look forward to our next collaboration.

- My good friend Rosemary Duffey, who—when I didn't like any of the available script fonts for the word "Abiding" on the cover—said, "You have nice handwriting; why don't you write it yourself?" Rose, that was such an Enneagram One suggestion for you to make, and for me to jump on. What would I do without you?

- Everyone whose stories appear in this book. I used real names with permission, except from those already in the world to come. I used pseudonyms sparingly, either at the request of the subject or because I could no longer find the person in question. Thank you all for allowing the particulars of your lives to illuminate my own.

- Sister Maria DeMonte, OP. Bless you for making me find another way to do the work. Rest in peace.
- Elysabeth Gelesky, Pilates for All Seasons. Thank you for strengthening my core, increasing my range of motion, and preventing me from losing precious writing hours to back injury.
- My "Happier Hour" ladies: Stephanie Fratantaro, Kati McMahon, RSM, Betsy Stone Plummer, and Marian Uba. Your extraordinary, enduring friendship has encouraged me greatly for decades. I'm so glad we're still together.
- My dear friend Deb Dunbar, who lives The Lesson of the Peaches every day. You have been such a steady cheerleader throughout this book process, while also saving a swath of Philadelphia from COVID-19. Our early-morning chats help me figure out how to be a better human being.
- My brother, Stephen. Thank you for enduring all the fuss about your sister being a published author, for promoting my work publicly while keeping me humble privately, for providing endless material for book chapters, for loving me unconditionally, and for marrying such a swell guy.

- My brother-in-law, John. Thank you for multiplying the joy, laughter, and profound conversation in my ordinary days. You are family forever and I love you.
- Porter, my dear. When my last book was published, you were working full-time; now you're retired and busier than ever. While serving as an Ignatian Volunteer at Sanctuary Farm, you still manage to be the roadie, chauffeur, and oftentimes caterer for the Christine show. Our frequent retreats to Maine are like oxygen for my soul. Thank you for helping to create a life in which this new freelance adventure can thrive.

Works Cited

Here If You Need Me: A True Story, by Kate Braestrup. New York: Little, Brown and Company, 2007.

This Flowing Toward Me: A Story of God Arriving in Strangers by Marilyn Lacey, R.S.M. Notre Dame: Ave Maria Press, 2009.

King, Charlie. "Our Life is More than Our Work" from the album *40 Songs for 40 Years*, CD Baby 2013.

Lewis, C. S. *Surprised by Joy: The Shape of My Early Life.* London: Geoffrey Blis, 1955.

Loyola, St. Ignatius. "The Daily Examen" at https://www.ignatianspirituality.com/ignatian-prayer/the-examen/

Loyola, St. Ignatius. "Suscipe" at https://www.ignatianspirituality.com/ignatian-prayer/prayers-by-st-ignatius-and-others/suscipe-the-radical-prayer/

Oliver, Mary. "You Never Know Where a Conversation is Going to Go," in *Dog Songs: Poems.* New York: Penguin Books, 2013.

Richardson, Jane. *Sparrow: A Book of Life and Death and Life* at www.janrichardson.com. Orlando: Wanton Gospeller Press, 2020.

Rilke, Rainer Maria. *Letters to a Young Poet.* New York: W. W. Norton & Company. 1934.

Woolf, Virginia. *A Room of One's Own.* London: Hogarth Press, 1929.

Pirkei Avot 2, Jewish Mishnah.